Original title:
Starlit Winter

Copyright © 2024 Swan Charm
All rights reserved.

Author: Kene Elistrand
ISBN HARDBACK: 978-9908-52-116-9
ISBN PAPERBACK: 978-9908-52-117-6
ISBN EBOOK: 978-9908-52-118-3

## Cosmic Chill of the Night

In the silence, stars awake,
Whispers of the moonlight speak.
Chill air wraps the world in peace,
Night unfolds, the day must cease.

Dreams drift softly on the breeze,
Lost beneath the towering trees.
Constellations paint the dark,
Each a story, each a spark.

Time stands still in twilight's glow,
Gentle waves of night flows slow.
The cosmos hums a serene tune,
Cradling hearts beneath the moon.

Shadows dance, the world in trance,
Every glance a fleeting chance.
Embrace the calm, let go of dread,
In this quiet, dreams are fed.

Beneath the vast and watchful skies,
Stars twinkle, as the night sighs.
With every breath, the chill ignites,
In cosmic chill, we find our sights.

## The Luminescent Frost of Dreams

Frosty tendrils lace the dawn,
Each glimmered gem a wish reborn.
Underneath the icy veil,
Dreams awaken with a tale.

In this shimmering white embrace,
Whispers dance in tranquil space.
Every crystal holds a plight,
Secrets hidden in the light.

Glistening pathways beckon near,
The heart ignites, emotions clear.
Frozen wishes, pure and bright,
Chasing shadows, welcoming light.

The landscape glows in silvery hues,
A canvas fresh for every muse.
Each breath a cloud of hope anew,
In frost, the dreams begin to stew.

Nights unfold, the stars align,
Frosty dreams in soft design.
A luminescent quilt of night,
Wraps our thoughts in crisp delight.

## Journey under the Velvet Sky

Beneath the cloak of velvet night,
We wander where the stars are bright.
Footsteps soft on whispering ground,
In this stillness, magic's found.

Galaxies spin, a cosmic dance,
Every heartbeat holds a chance.
With every glance, the infinite sighs,
Our spirits soar in the vast skies.

In the shadows, secrets gleam,
Every moment, a waking dream.
With the moon as our guiding light,
We embark on this wondrous flight.

Time dissolves in twilight's grace,
Faces change in this vast space.
Together, we chase the celestial gleams,
In the journey woven with dreams.

As horizons blend to deep blue,
We find ourselves, me and you.
Under the velvet sky so wide,
We wander free with hearts as guide.

# Whispers from a Crystal Universe

In the quiet void of night,
Stars shimmer with a gentle light.
Galaxies twirl in silver lace,
Whispers echo in this vast space.

Comets trace their fleeting dreams,
Through cosmic rivers, endless streams.
Each twinkling spark a tale to tell,
In this universe where wonders dwell.

Nebulas bloom in vibrant hues,
Softly painting the sky with views.
Celestial bodies dance and spin,
Inviting the heart to look within.

Amongst the silence, secrets hide,
In every corner, worlds abide.
The whispers of space, ancient and wise,
Guide longing hearts to distant skies.

So listen close, to the night's embrace,
And find your place in the starry chase.
For in the darkness, beauty is found,
In whispers soft, in cosmic sound.

# Luminescence Nestled in Chill

Winter wraps the world in white,
Beneath the moon's soft, glowing light.
Frosted trees stand tall and proud,
Clad in diamonds, wrapped like a shroud.

Every breath forms a misty cloud,
Nature sleeps beneath a silvery shroud.
Stars twinkle in the frosty air,
Whispers of magic linger everywhere.

Candles flicker, warming the nights,
In the hush, there are few delights.
A cozy hearth, the pulse of home,
In the chill, we are never alone.

Frozen rivers gently glide,
Beneath the ice, life does abide.
Snowflakes dance with a silent thrill,
In this realm of beauty, time stands still.

So cherish moments, soft and kind,
Embrace the stillness, peace you'll find.
In every flicker, each chilly gleam,
Luminescence whispers of a dream.

## **Whispers of Frosted Nights**

Underneath the starry sky,
The frosty air begins to sigh.
Whispers float on midnight's breath,
Casting shadows that flirt with death.

Winds weave tales through icy trees,
Carrying secrets on the freeze.
A symphony of quiet sounds,
Where stillness and mystery abounds.

Moonlight glimmers on the snow,
Painting paths where dreamers go.
Each crunch underfoot, a song,
Inviting us to linger long.

In the cold, our hearts aglow,
Sharing stories from long ago.
Frosted nights wrap us tight,
In whispers soft, we find our light.

So gather close, beneath night's veil,
Let the frost lead us down the trail.
For in this magic, together we'll find,
The whispers of dreams intertwined.

## **Celestial Snowfall**

Snowflakes drift from heavens high,
Dancing gently, they whisper why.
Each flake a story, unique and pure,
In their descent, a moment to cure.

Falling softly on the ground,
Covering all with a muffled sound.
Winter's quilt, serene and wide,
In its embrace, joy cannot hide.

Underneath the sky's vast dome,
Every flake whispers of home.
Gentle flakes touch every heart,
Binding us in this winter's art.

As the world fades into white,
Shivers warmed by firelight.
Quiet moments shared in bliss,
Celestial snowfall, wrapped in a kiss.

In this stillness, find your way,
Let the snow lead you astray.
For in each flake's soft, gentle fall,
Lies the magic that binds us all.

## **Temptations in Glacial Luminescence**

In the quiet glow of frost,
Whispers dance upon the ice.
Shadows glide with light embossed,
Silent beauty, paradise.

Stars above in velvet skies,
Casting dreams on glimmering trails.
Hearts awaken, filled with sighs,
Tempted by the night's soft tales.

Frozen realms of crystal bright,
Secrets held in winter's breath.
Every moment feels so right,
Chasing whispers, far from death.

Nature's breath in frigid air,
Calling souls to wander free.
Glacial lumens, rare and rare,
Temptations wild as they can be.

When the dawn begins to rise,
Hope emerges from the cold.
In each heartbeat, still and wise,
Lies the warmth of stories told.

## Cosmic Paths through Snowy Pines

Beneath the boughs where silence dwells,
Starlit paths beckon and shine.
In each shadow, a secret tells,
Guiding dreams through snowy pines.

Footsteps crunch where winter reigns,
Echoes dance in moonlit beams.
Cosmic wonders weave their chains,
As we walk through breathless dreams.

Frost-kissed air, a gentle thrill,
Whispers swirl in frosty curls.
Every heartbeat, a frozen chill,
In the heart of chilly swirls.

The universe unfolds above,
Stars align in tranquil grace.
Every tree a tale of love,
In the quiet, we embrace.

Nature's art in snowy glade,
Invites us to lose our way.
In the magic, hope is laid,
Through these paths, forever stay.

## Glacial Dreams of a Starry Night

Underneath a sky of dreams,
Where the glaciers softly sigh.
Starlight dances, softly gleams,
On the waves of night gone by.

Fragments of the world unfold,
In the silence, stories flow.
Whispers of the young and old,
In the night's ethereal glow.

Crystals spark in silver streams,
Flowing through the midnight air.
Guardians of our secret dreams,
Glistening jewels beyond compare.

In this glacial world we share,
Time suspends its timeless flight.
Lost in wonder, hearts laid bare,
Embracing glacial dreams tonight.

Hold this magic, never cease,
Let it linger, softly weave.
In the arms of frozen peace,
We find solace, we believe.

## **Elysium Wrapped in Winter's Embrace**

In the hushed embrace of night,
Winter drapes her silken veil.
Cradled in the soft moonlight,
Elysium whispers, hearts exhale.

Every flake a fleeting wish,
Landing softly on the ground.
In the cold, we find our bliss,
Wrapped in love that knows no bound.

Bare branches clothed in white gowns,
Guarding secrets of the past.
Through the pines, no trace of frowns,
In this stillness, joy is cast.

Winter's breath, a tender kiss,
Fills the air with pure delight.
In each moment, perfect bliss,
Elysium shines through the night.

As we wander hand in hand,
Time slows down in twilight's glow.
In this magic, love has planned,
Winter's beauty, free to flow.

## Astral Paths Through Frozen Whispers

Stars align in silent grace,
Guiding dreams through endless space.
Whispers float on icy winds,
Where every journey softly begins.

Beneath the quilt of starlit skies,
Hope ignites as nightbirds rise.
A cosmic dance of hidden light,
Leading hearts through the silent night.

Echoes swirl in the frosted air,
Magic lingers, serene and rare.
The universe hums a gentle tune,
Drawing souls 'neath the harvest moon.

In the chill where shadows blend,
New adventures eagerly transcend.
Paths unknown, yet brightly glowed,
Through frozen whispers, faith bestowed.

So take my hand in this embrace,
Together, let us find our place.
With every step, we'll cherish dreams,
Along astral paths and silver streams.

## An Ode to the Celestial Chill

Moonlight drapes the world in white,
A tranquil spell, a soothing sight.
Stars like diamonds, cold and pure,
In this frozen realm, our hearts endure.

Frosty breaths paint the air so clear,
Each exhale carries, far and near.
A symphony of ice and snow,
Whispers of winter in twilight's glow.

Celestial wonders, vast and bright,
Illuminate the canvas of night.
In silence, we find our way,
Through the chill of this mystical fray.

An ode to the beauty, bold and still,
In every corner where dreams fulfill.
The heavens smile, as shadows dance,
In the embrace of a cosmic trance.

So let us wander hand in hand,
Through winter's heart, a frozen land.
In every glimmer, a story unfolds,
Crafted in chill, in celestial molds.

## Silver Glimmers and Twinkling Lights

Silver glimmers on the lake,
Mirroring dreams where shadows wake.
Twinkling lights across the night,
Guide us gently towards the light.

In the hush of frost-kissed air,
Every breath is a whispered prayer.
Stars above in perfect line,
Remind us life is simply divine.

The world adorned in glistening frost,
In this journey, we find what's lost.
With every shimmer, hope ignites,
Illuminating hidden sights.

Crickets sing their soft goodbyes,
While the moon winks from the skies.
A tapestry of dusk unfolds,
Woven in silver threads of gold.

So dance beneath the cosmic glow,
Let your inner visions flow.
With every light, a wish takes flight,
In silver glimmers, hearts unite.

**Frosty Nights, Ethereal Sight**

On frosty nights the stillness grows,
As nature dons her sparkling clothes.
Ethereal sights enchant our gaze,
In the magic of winter's haze.

Whispers drift on flurries light,
Carrying secrets of the night.
In shadows, dreams begin to form,
A world reborn through winter's storm.

Stars like lanterns in the deep,
Awake our souls from tranquil sleep.
In their glow, we find our way,
Through the frost, where spirits play.

Each moment frozen, time stands still,
As nightingale sings with utmost thrill.
Beneath the veil of silvery light,
We dance together, pure delight.

So cherish every frosty breath,
In this embrace, we conquer death.
For in these nights, our hearts take flight,
As love ignites in ethereal sight.

## Dreams Adrift in the Arctic Glow

In shadows soft, the whispers play,
Where icy winds begin to sway.
Bold dreams float on frosty streams,
Wrapped in the warmth of silent dreams.

A blanket of stars, shimmering white,
Guides wandering hearts through the night.
With every breath, secrets unfold,
In the embrace of the bitter cold.

Ancient tales in the twilight weave,
Where gazes linger, and hearts believe.
Each flake a wish, a fleeting spark,
As thoughts drift forth in the Arctic dark.

Among the peaks, shadows dance and twist,
In the hush of an icy mist.
The glow of auroras paints the sky,
While dreams ignite and softly fly.

Beneath the stars, old hopes take flight,
Guided by the pale moonlight.
In this realm where wonders flow,
We'll chase our dreams, as rivers glow.

## **Frosty Reveries Above**

Beneath the frost, the silence breathes,
In every flake, a memory weaves.
Gentle whispers in the night,
Unfurling stories of pure delight.

Moonlit shadows kiss the ground,
Where hidden dreams begin to sound.
In the chill of night's embrace,
We find our solace, our sacred space.

Stars above like diamonds gleam,
We drift away in twilight's dream.
Echoes soft, a serene tune,
A lullaby beneath the moon.

Winds of winter sing so clear,
As we gather hopes held dear.
With every chill that stings our skin,
A frosty reverie waits within.

Time stands still in the pale glow,
As quiet secrets silently flow.
In frosty realms, our spirits soar,
Lost in dreams forever more.

## **When Stars Drip like Icicles**

The night unfolds a canvas rare,
Where stars cascade like silver hair.
Each droplet holds a silent plea,
Whispers woven in harmony.

Icicles hang in cosmic dance,
Glistening under a tranquil trance.
Stories drip from the skies above,
Whispers wrapped in cosmic love.

With every drop, a wish takes flight,
Floating free in the velvet night.
As dreams entwine with celestial light,
We lose ourselves in the endless sight.

Beneath the glow, our hearts ignite,
Capturing wonders in sheer delight.
In glimmer and spark, we find our place,
Where magic dwells in the soft embrace.

Stars that drip, like tears from the past,
Remind us that moments never last.
Yet in their fall, we find our way,
As night and dreams together sway.

## Cosmic Whispers Upon Cold Air

In the chill of the midnight hour,
Cosmic whispers hold their power.
Breathe in the frost, let dreams arise,
As starlight dances in endless skies.

Gentle murmurs speak of fate,
In winter's grasp, we contemplate.
With each exhale, a vision clear,
Stories shared, we draw them near.

Celestial songs beneath the stars,
A melody that transcends the scars.
With every note, a longing sigh,
Where time stands still and spirits fly.

Among the snowflakes, truths are found,
As cosmic echoes swirl around.
In cold embrace, we feel the spark,
Of dreams igniting in the dark.

So listen close, let your soul unwind,
In the whispers, your heart will find.
Among the stars, love's radiant flare,
In cosmic whispers upon cold air.

## The Winter Sky's Serenade

The whispers of snowflakes fall,
Dancing under a silver sprawl.
Moonlight bathes the silent ground,
In this peace, dreams are found.

Trees glisten with a frosty sheen,
Nature wrapped in a soft routine.
Wind carries a gentle tune,
Underneath the glowing moon.

Stars twinkle in the vast expanse,
Inviting all in a timeless dance.
Each glitter a story untold,
In this night, magic unfolds.

Time slows in the cold embrace,
Heartbeats quiet in this place.
Breath forms clouds that softly drift,
As the sky offers its gift.

The winter sky sings, so high,
In its depths, our spirits fly.
With every note, the air feels bright,
In this serenade of night.

## Galactic Trails on Snowy Paths

Footprints lead through the silent wood,
Marking where the wanderers stood.
Galactic trails on the snow's crust,
Whispers of dreams in the starlit dust.

Radiant beams through branches weave,
A tapestry that all souls believe.
The night sky, a canvas of grace,
Inviting all to find their place.

Crisp air holds the stories of old,
In the shimmer, the secrets unfold.
Echoes of laughter linger near,
Filling the night with warmth and cheer.

Each step echoes in pure delight,
Guided by stars, we ignite.
The snowy paths beneath our feet,
A memory of every heartbeat.

Together we travel, hand in hand,
In this magical winter land.
Galactic whispers call us home,
Under this sky, we freely roam.

## Celestial Wishes on Frosty Ridge

On frosty ridge, where silence reigns,
With each breath, our hope remains.
Celestial wishes float like dreams,
In a world that glistens and gleams.

Stars sprinkle blessings from above,
Wrapping the night in timeless love.
Moonlit moments share their grace,
As we pause in this sacred space.

Frosty winds whisper secrets near,
Carried gently for hearts that hear.
In the hush of the midnight air,
We find peace resting everywhere.

Hand in hand, we watch and wait,
For the magic of the night to elevate.
Each shooting star, a wish we send,
Reaching far, where dreams transcend.

In the glow of the twilight hour,
We embrace the night's twinkling power.
Frosty ridge beams with light so bright,
Celestial wishes take their flight.

## The Chill of Stars Above

The chill of night is crisp and clear,
Stars emerge, drawing us near.
In the vastness, we gaze with awe,
Each shimmer a mystery that we draw.

Beneath the canopy of endless skies,
We marvel at the world's reply.
The constellations guide our way,
In their brilliance, night turns to day.

Frostbitten wind nips at our skin,
Yet warmth ignites from within.
In the quiet, dreams take flight,
Soaring high in this endless night.

The chill of stars weaves through our hearts,
In each twinkle, a story starts.
With whispered hopes, we reach so high,
In this dark, we learn to fly.

Together we sit, in wonder and peace,
Warmed by the glow that will never cease.
The chill of stars will always stay,
Guiding us gently, come what may.

## Crystals Catching Cosmic Light

In the depths of night, they glow bright,
With colors dancing, pure delight.
Each shard a star, a cosmic spark,
Whispers of dreams in the dark.

The universe sings in every hue,
A symphony of light, forever true.
Fragile beauty, strong and wise,
Reflecting wonders from the skies.

They shimmer softly, in silence they sway,
Guiding lost souls along their way.
Crystals gleaming, hearts take flight,
Catching echoes of cosmic light.

Beneath the moon, they come alive,
In their presence, hopes revive.
A tale of ages written in stone,
In the glow of crystals, we're never alone.

Forever etched in the sky's embrace,
They hold memories, time cannot erase.
In their facets, life reflects,
Crystals catching cosmic effects.

## **Vows Made in Frost and Flame**

Amidst the frost, a whisper shared,
In icy breath, the hearts have bared.
Flames flicker with an ardent glow,
Binding souls in a dance, aglow.

Promises wrapped in the chill of night,
Where embers burn with passionate light.
Each vow sealed with a gentle touch,
Frost and flame, we cherish much.

Fire dances with the frost's embrace,
In their clash, we find our place.
Love ignited in wintry air,
With every vow, we become a pair.

With diamond snowflakes as our witness,
Together we navigate the fitness.
In the warmth of flame, the cold retreats,
Forging bonds that love completes.

Through seasons shift, our vows remain,
In frost and flame, love knows no pain.
An eternal dance, through storm and calm,
In every heart, we find our balm.

## The Canvas of Cosmic White

Upon the canvas, white and pure,
Stars are painted, soft allure.
Each stroke a dream, a journey spun,
In the embrace of night, we run.

Swirling galaxies within our sight,
In this cosmic vastness, hearts take flight.
Gentle hues of silver and gray,
Canvas brightens as night meets day.

Snowflakes fall, a gentle sigh,
Kissing the earth with every high.
In quiet wonder, we find our way,
The canvas whispers, come what may.

Infinite wonders, secrets untold,
The universe's stories unfold.
In the stillness, we paint our fate,
Colors merging, we contemplate.

A masterpiece made of hopes and dreams,
Echoing life in sparkling streams.
Canvas of white, a world anew,
In every heartbeat, we are few.

## Magic in the Moonlit Breeze

Underneath the silver skies,
A world awakens, magic flies.
Whispers carried on the night air,
In the breeze, dreams softly stir.

Moonbeams dance on tranquil seas,
Every sigh a spell, a tease.
With every ripple, hearts align,
In this moment, the stars entwine.

Laughter echoes in shadows cast,
Time pauses, present meets the past.
Magic weaves through every leaf,
A gentle touch, beyond belief.

With every breath, the night expands,
Holding secrets in tender hands.
In the breeze, our spirits soar,
Magic abounds, forevermore.

As dawn approaches, we hold tight,
To the spells spun in the night.
In the moonlit breeze, we find our song,
In every heartbeat, we belong.

# A Serenade Beneath the Constellations

In the stillness of night, we gaze,
Stars whisper softly, lost in a haze.
Each twinkle a tale of distant dreams,
Carried by winds, or so it seems.

Moonlight dances on your face,
Painting shadows, a gentle grace.
Hearts in rhythm, harmonized beats,
Under the cosmos, our souls meet.

The sky unfolds like a lover's sigh,
Infinite wonders, where secrets lie.
With each breath, the universe sighs,
In this moment, time softly flies.

We find solace in the gentle glow,
A serenade sung, soft and slow.
Each note a promise, tender and true,
In this embrace, it's just us two.

As constellations weave their art,
The cosmos cradles my beating heart.
Together we wander, hand in hand,
Lost in the magic of this celestial land.

## **Chilling Radiance of the Night**

Beneath the moon's chilling, silver light,
Shadows whisper secrets, taking flight.
Frosty air tingles on my skin,
Welcome silence, where thoughts begin.

The stars are diamonds, cold yet bright,
Glimmering softly in the velvet night.
Each breath a cloud that dances away,
In this embrace, I long to stay.

Frozen branches creak and sway,
Memories echo from yesterday.
A hush falls gently over the land,
In this stillness, I understand.

The night wraps close like a woven cloak,
Holding warmth in every lingering stroke.
Time stands still, a tranquil sea,
In the moon's embrace, it's just you and me.

With every glance, we find our ease,
In the chilling radiance, hearts appease.
The world fades out, it's just our light,
Together we shine, in the depth of night.

## Frosted Echoes in the Dark

In shadows deep, the frost takes hold,
Whispers of winter, stories untold.
Echoes linger in the biting air,
A symphony played, tender and rare.

Each breath released, a frosty plume,
Stars above twinkle, dispelling gloom.
The world shimmers in silvery shades,
In the silence, my spirit cascades.

Footsteps crunch on the frozen ground,
A melody woven in the quiet sound.
Darkness envelops, yet feels so near,
In the chill, my heart lays bare.

Whispers of night seep through the trees,
Carried on currents of frosty breeze.
In every flicker, a story unfolds,
Of love and longing in winter's cold.

In this darkness, a beauty bright,
Frosted echoes guiding my sight.
Through layers of cold, warmth I find,
In the depths of night, our souls entwined.

# Twilight's Embrace on Glacial Shores

Twilight descends with a soft, warm touch,
Golden hues quench the shadows' clutch.
Glacial shores, where the land meets sea,
Whispers of twilight, wild and free.

Colors blend in a gentle caress,
Night-draped silence, a soothing dress.
The horizon stretches, kissed by the sun,
In this moment, we are all as one.

Waves murmur secrets from the deep,
Promises carried where dreams sleep.
Twilight unfolds like a tender story,
Endings and beginnings wrapped in glory.

We wander close, hearts intertwined,
In twilight's embrace, our fates aligned.
Each glance shared ignites a spark,
Guided together, though the world is dark.

As night takes hold, stars pierce the sky,
Twilight whispers, a soft lullaby.
On glacial shores, our spirits soar,
In this serene moment, we are forevermore.

## **Celestial Whispers of Frost**

In the hush of the night,
Whispers dance through the air.
Frosty breath gently glows,
Stars twinkle with care.

Crystals cling to the pines,
Nature's wonder unfurls.
Delicate lace on the ground,
A blanket of pearls.

Moonlight spills like a dream,
Swirling shadows unite.
Each step crunches softly,
In the deep, quiet night.

The world breathes a still song,
Echoing under the frost.
Beauty rare, pure, and calm,
In a moment, it's lost.

Celestial secrets wait,
In the stillness of time.
Frost whispers to the stars,
In rhythm and rhyme.

**Velvet Skies and Crystal Dreams**

Beneath velvet skies so vast,
Dreams weave through the night.
Stars like jewels shimmer bright,
   Casting a magical light.

The moon hangs low and full,
   A guardian of night's grace.
Embracing all secrets kept,
   In this enchanted space.

Whispers of the evening breeze,
   Carry tales from afar.
Each breath a story unfolds,
   Beneath the guiding star.

Crystals gleam on the ground,
   Mirroring heavens high.
Nature's elegant embrace,
   As the night drifts by.

In this realm of soft dreams,
Hearts find their peace and rest.
Velvet skies cradle hope,
   In a night blessed.

## When Night Falls on the Snow

When night falls on the snow,
A hush envelopes the land.
Each flake a silent story,
Crafted by winter's hand.

Footprints lead into dark,
Guided by the moon's glow.
Whispers echo through the trees,
As the world moves slow.

Shadows stretch and yawn wide,
Blankets of white unfold.
Stars scatter like secrets,
In the midnight cold.

A chill wraps around hearts,
Under blankets of dreams.
When night falls on the snow,
Everything softly gleams.

The tranquil beauty sways,
In the glimmering night.
Peace drapes over the earth,
In the soft silver light.

## **Moonbeams on Icy Silence**

Moonbeams touch icy ground,
A soft glow in the still.
Silence wrapped in crystal,
As dreams begin to fill.

The world shimmers and sleeps,
Underneath a shroud of white.
Echoes of a whispered past,
Flow gently through the night.

Each shadow tells a tale,
Carried forth by the wind.
Icy silence wraps all tight,
As mysteries rescind.

Stars glimmer in the dark,
Guiding souls lost in thought.
Moonbeams caress the silence,
In the magic time bought.

The night breathes soft and slow,
A lullaby of frost.
In this moment of peace,
All worries are lost.

## Chasing the Comet's Tail

Across the night, we run so free,
With dreams that soar like birds from trees.
A streak of light in the vast dark sky,
We chase the comet, you and I.

The echoes of laughter, faint but near,
In moments shared, we shed our fear.
With every leap, we defy the night,
Holding on tight, to pure delight.

The trail it leaves, a memory bright,
Guiding us through the starry light.
In the wake of wonder, we find our way,
To hopes reborn with each new day.

Time may scatter like leaves in the breeze,
Yet in this chase, our hearts find ease.
Together we'll spell the tales untold,
As we grasp at dreams, vivid and bold.

So let us dance in this cosmic play,
With spirits high, we'll joyfully sway.
For in the wake of the comet's flight,
We'll forge our path in endless night.

## Silhouettes Under Twinkling Stars

Beneath the arch of indigo hue,
We sit in silence, just me and you.
With whispers soft like a gentle breeze,
In the night's embrace, our hearts find ease.

The stars above, a shimmering sight,
Casting glow over dreams of the night.
In silhouettes, our stories blend,
An endless dance, without an end.

With the moon as our only guide,
We wander where the dreams reside.
Together, cherished moments grow,
In the starlit realm, where wishes flow.

The cosmos hums a haunting tune,
In balance with the wistful moon.
In twilight's warmth, time stands still,
While shadows stretch, and hearts fulfill.

So let's make wishes upon those stars,
And paint our dreams, from near to far.
For under these twinkling skies we find,
The love that binds us, forever entwined.

## Winter's Ethereal Embrace

Snowflakes fall like whispers soft,
In winter's hold, we drift aloft.
A blanket white, the world is still,
In tranquil beauty, hearts we fill.

The trees stand bare, yet dressed in grace,
With frost-kissed limbs, they hold their place.
In silence deep, we find our breath,
In winter's arms, we dance with death.

The chill creeps in, a tender shroud,
Yet love ignites, fierce and proud.
With every glance, the warmth we chase,
As we twirl in winter's sweet embrace.

The night descends, a tranquil balm,
With stars aligned, it feels like calm.
Together here, we share the fire,
In winter's heart, we find desire.

So let us wander, hand in hand,
Through frosted fields and snow-clad land.
In every flake, a tender trace,
Of winter's love, an endless grace.

## A Dance of Snowflakes and Stars

In the night sky, stars twinkle bright,
As snowflakes swirl, a magical sight.
An orchestra of dreams takes flight,
With whispers soft, we share our delight.

The ground adorned in purest white,
Beneath our feet, the world feels light.
With every step, we weave our song,
In harmony where we both belong.

The moon's soft glow reflects our glee,
As we dance together, wild and free.
Lost in the moment, the world fades away,
In this celestial ballet, we sway.

Stars above like diamonds rare,
Guide us gently through the cold air.
With laughter bright, we spin and twirl,
As magic dances, like a swirl.

In this embrace of night and snow,
We find a peace that starts to grow.
In the dance of snowflakes, stars align,
A bond of love, sacred and divine.

## Twilight's Promise of Sparkling Grace

In twilight's glow, the stars ignite,
A whisper soft, a gentle light.
Promises dance on evening's breeze,
Graceful shadows sway like trees.

The horizon blushes, paints the skies,
With hues that lull and mesmerize.
A tapestry of dreams unfurls,
As night embraces the sleeping pearls.

## When Seasons Merge with the Cosmos

When spring meets fall in vibrant fight,
The colors clash, a vivid sight.
Leaves of gold and blooms so bright,
A cosmic ballet, pure delight.

Stars align with blooms in flight,
As nature sings in purest rite.
Each season's call, a whispered tune,
Under the watchful eye of the moon.

## **Starry Veil Over Crystal Land**

A crystal land beneath starlit skies,
Whispers of magic, where wonder lies.
The night unfolds with shimmering grace,
A starry veil, a timeless embrace.

In silence deep, the echoes sing,
Of hidden dreams that shadows bring.
Celestial dance across the plains,
Where time stands still and hope remains.

## Hushed Secrets of the Winter Sky

Beneath the hush of winter's breath,
The sky reveals its tales of death.
In frosty air, the secrets flow,
As starlit wonders softly glow.

Snowflakes twirl like whispered sighs,
Each one crafted beneath dark skies.
A quilt of white cloaks the earth's embrace,
In winter's grip, we find our place.

## **Glittering Trails of Frozen Light**

In the still of winter nights,
Footprints glimmer on the snow,
Whispers dance in moonlit sights,
Where the gentle breezes blow.

Stars above like diamonds gleam,
Casting shadows soft and bright,
In the dreamer's silent dream,
Glittering trails of frozen light.

Each step leads to magic's call,
A path where time seems to suspend,
Nature's beauty, pure enthrall,
In this world, where dreams transcend.

Beneath the canopy of night,
Hope and wonder intertwine,
In the heart, a spark ignites,
Guided by a fate divine.

As dawn breaks, the glimmers fade,
Yet the memory lingers near,
In the stillness, dreams we made,
Shimmer on, forever clear.

## The Silence of Starry Evenings

In the hush of twilight's glow,
Stars awake, a soft embrace,
Whispers of the night bestow,
A tranquil heart, a quiet space.

Moonlight bathes the world in silver,
Gentle breezes lift the sighs,
Nature's song begins to quiver,
Underneath the sprawling skies.

Each twinkle tells a story old,
Of dreams and hopes long gone astray,
In the beauty, we behold,
The silent night will lead the way.

Harmony in stillness found,
As shadows cast their soothing veil,
In this peace, we are unbound,
In this night, our souls set sail.

The silence wraps around like lace,
Embracing every whispered thought,
In the dark, we find our place,
In the stillness, love is sought.

## Luminous Dreams on Frosty Grains

On the fields where frost has kissed,
Morning glories softly gleam,
In the air, a quiet mist,
Crafting visions, born of dream.

Grains of frost like tiny stars,
Scatter light with every sway,
In the softness, peace is ours,
As the dawn begins to play.

Every step on icy ground,
Leaves behind a tale untold,
In this moment, we have found,
Luminous dreams in colors bold.

With each breath, the world awakes,
In the hush of early morn,
Nature's canvas softly shapes,
Visions vibrant and reborn.

As the sun begins to rise,
Lifting shadows from the deep,
In this light, our spirits rise,
In frosty grains, our dreams we keep.

## A Blanket of Twinkles on the Ground

Upon the earth, a soft embrace,
A blanket woven bright at night,
Stars descend and softly grace,
The world below with twinkling light.

Each glimmer speaks of distant lands,
Of tales that whisper on the breeze,
In the silence of the strands,
We find solace, hearts at ease.

Moonbeams lace through trees that sway,
Creating shadows long and thin,
In this quiet, dreams shall play,
Awakening the joys within.

Beneath this sky, we cast our fears,
For in the dark, we learn to see,
With every star that appears,
A blueprint of what could be.

In the midnight hush profound,
The universe sings its song,
Wrapped in twinkles on the ground,
We find the place where we belong.

## Frost-Kissed Nocturne

In the hush of night, frost lays,
Crystals twinkle, icy rays,
Underneath the silver moon,
Whispers echo, soft as tunes.

Trees adorned in gleaming white,
Silent guardians of the night,
Footsteps muffled, dreams awake,
Nature's peace, a tender ache.

Stars above, in velvet skies,
Glisten bright, like hopeful sighs,
A serenade, the cold winds sing,
Bringing joy, winter's blessing.

Shadows dance in soft moonlight,
Frosted branches hold on tight,
A moment paused in time's embrace,
Finding warmth in nature's grace.

Time flows gently, soft and slow,
In this wonderland of snow,
Hearts align in quiet throng,
To the rhythm of night's song.

## Ethereal Glow on Snowbound Paths

Dancing lights on snowy trails,
Nature's brush through moonlit veils,
Each step gives a gentle spark,
Guiding souls through the dark.

Frosted branches lightly sway,
In the stillness of the tray,
Whispers carried by the breeze,
Bringing comfort, hearts at ease.

Veils of shimmer, soft and pale,
Secrets held in silent tales,
As the night embraces all,
Ethereal glow, a soft call.

Every flake a dream untold,
In the grasp of winter's hold,
Paths of silver, winding low,
Leading us where hopes can grow.

In this realm of pure delight,
Where the stars twinkle bright,
We find our place, our way to roam,
In the magic, we feel at home.

## Secrets Linger in the Cold

In the chill, the secrets hide,
Underneath the winter's tide,
Frosty breath on whispered breeze,
Tales of old, the heart agrees.

Beneath the snow, where dreams lie still,
Nature's pulse, a tranquil thrill,
Echoes of the past abide,
In the twilight, shadows bide.

Moonlight casting silvery sheens,
Through the trees, in tangled scenes,
Whispers travel through the night,
Secrets linger, out of sight.

Crystals form, a fragile art,
Embracing every wandering heart,
In the cold, the truth unfolds,
As the night-time magic holds.

Every breath a soft refrain,
As silence weaves through frost and grain,
In the winter's clutch, we find,
The secrets of the heart, entwined.

## Celestial Frost and Whispering Pines

Under stars, the frosty pines,
Whisper tales of ancient signs,
Celestial glow upon the ground,
Magic lingers all around.

Silver needles catch the light,
In the quiet of the night,
Every rustle, soft and clear,
Nature's language, drawing near.

Frozen ponds in glassy sheen,
Reflecting worlds so pure, serene,
Moments pause, each heartbeat sways,
Lost in winter's gentle ways.

Frosty breaths and gleaming skies,
In the stillness, spirit flies,
Beneath the boughs, we feel the grace,
Of every dream in this embrace.

Winter's canvas, vast and wide,
Awakens wonder, never hides,
With every whisper, every sigh,
Celestial frost, our hearts comply.

## Crystalline Stars in December's Lap

In the quiet of night,
The stars twinkle bright,
A tapestry unfolds,
As winter's breath holds.

Glistening flakes descend,
Soft whispers they send,
Crystalline dreams swirl,
In a frosty twirl.

Each moment feels still,
Time bends to our will,
Under skies so deep,
Where secrets shall keep.

Moonlight kisses the ground,
In silence profound,
We dance with the night,
Chasing soft starlight.

December's heart glows,
As magic bestows,
A world draped in white,
Bathed in gentle light.

## **The Gentle Kiss of Northern Lights**

High above the trees,
A glow lingers free,
Waves of color flow,
Like whispers of snow.

Emerald and gold,
Stories untold,
Weaving through the sky,
Where wishes can fly.

In the cool night air,
There's magic to share,
As shadows embrace,
The night's warm grace.

Beneath the display,
We sway and we play,
Wrapped in nature's song,
Where we all belong.

With a soft caress,
The lights still impress,
Their dance on the dome,
Calls our hearts back home.

# Diaphanous Nightfall on Silver Streets

Silhouettes unfold,
As night's tale is told,
A hush lingers near,
Whispers calm our fear.

Moonbeams brush the ground,
While stars twirl around,
Cobblestones shimmer,
As old shadows glimmer.

Through the silver haze,
Time gently delays,
Each step feels divine,
In this space of mine.

The air softly sighs,
As twilight complies,
With secrets to share,
In the cool night air.

Diaphanous dreams rise,
Under starlit skies,
Each moment feels vast,
Yet will not hold fast.

## Ethereal Dance of Radiance Above

In the vast expanse,
Colors weave and prance,
An ethereal glow,
In the night below.

Stars orchestrate light,
In a choreographed flight,
A celestial show,
For our hearts to know.

The universe sways,
In celestial ways,
A tapestry spun,
From dusk until dawn.

As wonder ignites,
In the ethereal nights,
We twirl in embrace,
Lost in time and space.

With silence so sweet,
We find our heart's beat,
In a radiant sea,
Forever we'll be.

## The Night's Breath on Frozen Whispers

A chill hangs softly in the air,
The stars blink gently overhead.
Whispers of secrets, light as air,
In shadows where the dreams are fed.

The moon glows bright, a silver coin,
Casting its glow on sleepy lands.
Echoes of frost where hearts can join,
In silence where the beauty stands.

Footprints trace stories in the snow,
Each step a tale left behind.
The night's breath hums, a gentle flow,
A melody of worlds entwined.

In this embrace of soft twilight,
Waves of peace caress the mind.
Finding solace in the night,
Where every longing can unwind.

As dawn approaches, shadows fade,
The whispers yield to morning light.
But in the heart, the magic stayed,
A frozen breath, a dream in flight.

## Woven Dreams in the Glittering Cold

Through icy branches, fairies dance,
Their laughter sparkles in the night.
Woven dreams in a moonlit trance,
The world adorned in silver light.

Crystals glimmer on every branch,
Nature's jewels, a splendid sight.
The breeze begins its gentle branch,
As shadows whisper secrets bright.

Every flake a story spun,
Falling softly, never old.
Each creation, they have done,
Woven dreams in the glittering cold.

Together they paint a masterpiece,
A canvas born from winter's breath.
In this stillness, find your peace,
A quiet beauty, life from death.

So take my hand, let's dance tonight,
Underneath the starry skies.
In this world of pure delight,
Woven dreams that never die.

## Moonlit Skies and Silent Echoes

Beneath the veil of midnight skies,
The moonlight bathes the earth anew.
Silent echoes, whispered sighs,
In the stillness, time slips through.

A blanket soft of silver hue,
Cradles all of nature's sleep.
Stars twinkle like a chosen few,
In secrets that the nightwood keeps.

Moments pass like fleeting dreams,
Carried on the wings of night.
In the dark, the world redeems,
With moonlit paths that feel so right.

Guided by a million stars,
We wander where the shadows play.
No distance feels too vast or far,
In this calm, we find our way.

And when the sun begins to rise,
The echoes softly fade from sight.
But in our hearts, the moonlight lies,
A keeper of our silent night.

## **Frosted Stars Adorn the Dark**

In winter's chill, the stars arise,
Frosted gems upon the night.
They twinkle softly in the skies,
Adorn the dark with silver light.

The blanket deep of twinkling white,
Wraps the earth in a hushed embrace.
Underneath the vast, soft flight,
Dreams take shape in endless space.

The world feels hushed, a quiet sigh,
While shadows dance on frozen ground.
And in the cold, each heart beats high,
In wonder where the peace is found.

Through frosted branches, whispers flow,
Stories told of ages past.
Each flickering light begins to glow,
In that stillness, forever cast.

So let us gaze upon this night,
With hearts alight and spirits bright.
For in the dark, all things align,
Frosted stars, our hearts entwine.

## Dances of Light Across Frozen Fields

Whispers of dawn break the chill,
Shadows stretch, the world stands still.
Glistening flakes leap in delight,
As colors twirl in morning light.

Soft breezes weave through the trees,
Embracing whispers, gentle pleas.
Frosty petals, nature's art,
A symphony that warms the heart.

Golden rays kiss the crisp air,
Each breath, a story laid bare.
Beneath the sky, dreams take flight,
In dances of light, joy ignites.

As twilight cloaks the evening glow,
Stars awaken, their soft throw.
They shimmer down on fields below,
A tapestry of silver snow.

In the hush of night's embrace,
Eternal beauty finds its place.
Frozen fields, a world so bright,
In the dance, we take our flight.

## Under the Spell of a Bright Sky

Waves of azure, clouds drift past,
Moments slip away too fast.
Golden sunbeams chase the gray,
A canvas where the children play.

Butterflies flit with carefree grace,
In a world where time leaves no trace.
Joyful laughter fills the air,
Under the spell, hearts laid bare.

Beneath this dome of endless blue,
Nature sings a song so true.
Each petal blooms, each tree stands tall,
Whispers of wonder, a sweet call.

As shadows stretch and evening nears,
Stars awaken, calming fears.
The moon shines bright, a silver eye,
In the magic, we will fly.

Wrapped in dreams, we softly sway,
Chasing the shadows of the day.
Under the spell, forever stay,
In the light's warm, sweet ballet.

## **Celestial Patterns on the Silent Ground**

Stars above in perfect arrays,
Map the night in glittering ways.
Each twinkle tells a story old,
In celestial patterns, dreams unfold.

The silent earth beneath our feet,
Holds secrets wrapped in night's sweet sheet.
With each heartbeat, the whispers rise,
Echoing tales of endless skies.

Moonlight dances on the dew,
Painting shadows, silver hue.
A tranquil moment, time on hold,
Nature's wonders quietly told.

As time weaves through the velvet night,
Constellations share their light.
The universe, a grand display,
Guides us softly through our stay.

In the silence, hearts align,
Under stars that brightly shine.
Celestial patterns on the ground,
In their beauty, peace is found.

## **Frigid Murmurs from Beyond**

In the stillness, whispers flow,
Frigid murmurs from the snow.
They dance upon the frosty air,
Secrets of the winter bare.

Echoes of the past emerge,
Through frozen realms, memories surge.
Each breath a tale, each sigh a song,
In the cold, where we belong.

Nature's voice, a call so clear,
Wraps around us, draws us near.
Beneath the stars, the night so bold,
Dreams awaken, bright and cold.

Guided by the northern light,
We wander through the velvet night.
Frigid wonders in our wake,
Illuminating paths we take.

In chilly whispers, spirits speak,
In every shadow, solace seek.
Frigid murmurs from afar,
Lead us to where dreams are star.

## The Silence Where Winter Meets the Sky

The snowflakes drift, a gentle sigh,
In stillness felt, beneath the sky.
Whispers soft, the cold air breathes,
Nature holds its dream beneath steep eaves.

Pines stand tall in frosted grace,
Clad in white, a silent lace.
Stars emerge, their twinkle bright,
In quietude, the heart takes flight.

Moonlight spills on distant hills,
A silver cloak, the night instills.
Echoes roam in frosty air,
As winter's hush lays secrets bare.

The world retreats, yet life persists,
In icy grasp, it still exists.
Those moments calm, a sacred pause,
Nature sings without a cause.

In the air, a magic hum,
As winters come, and winters drum.
So here we stand, entranced in time,
Where silence reigns, and dreams can climb.

## **Lights Dancing in the Bitter Chill**

The stars ignite in frigid night,
A dance of lights, a wondrous sight.
Each flicker tells a tale untold,
In bitter chill, their beauty bold.

Beneath the moon's soft, watchful glow,
Frosted fields with secrets flow.
The air is crisp, it bites the skin,
Yet hearts are warm, and dreams begin.

As winter winds begin to swirl,
They weave through trees with a gentle twirl.
A symphony of nature sings,
In quiet night, the magic clings.

Dancing shadows play their game,
In the dark, we whisper names.
The icy breath of winter's song,
Binds us all, both weak and strong.

So hold me close in this embrace,
Where lights and chill bring joy and grace.
In every glimmer, hope is found,
In the bitter chill, love's warmth surrounds.

## **Keys to the Universe's Icy Heart**

The cosmos sleeps, in shadows deep,
Where icy secrets lie and keep.
A vault of stars, a frozen grin,
In winter's hush, new dreams begin.

Each twinkling light, a hidden key,
Unlocking worlds beyond the sea.
The frost-kissed air, a silent plea,
To delve beneath and set them free.

Galaxies spin in whispering night,
Each secret held in crystal light.
We search for meaning in the cold,
And find our stories waiting, bold.

The universe, with icy heart,
Invites us in, to play our part.
So listen close, the cosmos speaks,
In frozen breaths, the silence seeks.

With every star, a chance to soar,
In winter's arms, we are reborn.
Dreams take flight in cosmic space,
With keys to realms, we find our place.

**Frosted Horizons and Twinkling Dreams**

Horizon glows, a canvas bright,
In shades of blue and silver light.
Across the dawn, a chill remains,
Yet hope unfolds, and joy sustains.

The frost is soft on morning bloom,
A delicate touch that stirs the room.
Whispers of dreams take to the air,
In frosted hues, we find our care.

As daylight breaks, the world awakes,
In winter's breath, the heart then quakes.
Twinkling wonders dance in mind,
As stories of light begin to unwind.

Through valleys deep and mountains high,
The beauty calls, we cannot deny.
Each frosted breath, a prayer we weave,
In golden dawn, we dare believe.

With every step on this icy path,
We tread with grace, we seek the math.
Frosted horizons, dreams align,
In winter's chill, the stars refine.

## A Canvas of Frost Under Cosmic Light

Stars above twinkle bright,
Painting the night with dreams.
Whispers of ice in the air,
A world wrapped in silver beams.

Beneath the vast endless sky,
Snowflakes dance, a gentle sigh.
Nature's canvas, pure and clear,
Each frozen breath, a silent cheer.

Footprints trace a path so small,
Stories told in winter's hall.
With every step, the heart takes flight,
On this canvas of cosmic light.

A chill wraps around the trees,
Branches hold the frosty tease.
In the quiet, magic flows,
Under the glow, the wonder grows.

The moon, a guardian so bright,
Watches over this serene night.
A canvas of frost, a sight to see,
Cradled softly, wild and free.

## Winter's Breath and Celestial Secrets

In the hush of winter's breath,
Secrets linger, tales of depth.
Snowflakes whisper through the trees,
Carried softly on the freeze.

Celestial wonders shine above,
A universe of endless love.
Each twinkle holds a frozen wish,
In wintry air, dreams start to swish.

The ground is cloaked in white so deep,
In its quiet, the world does sleep.
Underneath the starry dome,
Winter sings a song of home.

Branches bare, yet spirits high,
Sculptures of ice, how they lie.
Flurries swirl in cosmic breeze,
Nature's art that aims to please.

Beneath the frost, the earth does lie,
Waiting for the sun to comply.
In winter's breath, the secrets keep,
A symphony in silence deep.

## Hushed Footprints Under Starlight

Night's embrace wraps all in peace,
With every breath, our worries cease.
Footprints leave a trace so light,
Guided gently by starlit sight.

In the stillness, time stands still,
Nature's heart, a soothing thrill.
The moon hangs low, a watchful eye,
Over dreams that take to the sky.

Each step whispers soft and clear,
Echoes of joy, the heart draws near.
The vast expanse, a velvet cloth,
Holding secrets time forgot.

Snowflakes twirl like dancers bright,
In this winter's magical night.
Hushed, we wander, hand in hand,
Across this white, enchanted land.

Under stars, our spirits soar,
Each moment cherished, forevermore.
With hushed footprints in the snow,
We carve out love where cold winds blow.

## Luminescent Tales in Shimmering Snow

In the glow of winter's light,
Snowflakes shimmer through the night.
Each one tells a tale untold,
Of ancient dreams in frosty gold.

The world transformed, a dreamland lies,
Underneath the starry skies.
Whispers of the past still sing,
In the hush that winter brings.

Every footprint, a story spun,
A dance beneath a frozen sun.
Luminescent magic weaves,
Snowy patterns, nature breathes.

Frozen rivers, ice-bound streams,
Carry echoes of our dreams.
The air is thick with lore and light,
In this realm of gentle night.

So let us walk, hand in hand,
Through this soft, enchanted land.
In luminescent tales, we find,
The beauty of the world's design.

## **Tapestry of Winter's Night**

The moon hangs low, a silver thread,
Whispers of frost on the earth's soft bed.
Pine trees sway, cloaked in white,
While shadows dance in the shimmering light.

Footsteps crunch on the icy ground,
Silence echoes, beauty profound.
Hush of the world in restful embrace,
Nature's canvas, a tranquil space.

Stars twinkle bright, like diamonds rare,
Each one a wish floating in cold air.
A blanket of dark, yet vivid and clear,
In winter's night magic, we draw near.

Breath of the night, crisp and cold,
Stories of warmth quietly told.
Frozen streams reflect the sky,
In winter's spell, we drift and fly.

So let us dance in this serene glow,
Wrapped in the warmth of falling snow.
Together we weave, in the moon's soft light,
A tapestry spun on winter's night.

## Aurora's Lullaby

In the hush of dawn, colors ignite,
Painting the sky with dreamlike light.
Whispers of green, pink, and gold,
Aurora's song, a tale retold.

Gentle waves in the chilly air,
Nature's symphony, beyond compare.
Stars fade slowly, they take their leave,
As the sun awakens, we believe.

Each light a promise, soft and bright,
Casting away shadows of the night.
Embracing the earth, a warm embrace,
In this twilight dance, we find our place.

Winds carry melodies from afar,
Guiding our hearts beneath the stars.
With every pulse, the world comes alive,
In this celestial glow, we thrive.

So let us linger in this soft glow,
Where night kisses day, and dreams may grow.
Together we'll sing, forever sway,
To Aurora's lullaby, brightening our way.

## **The Universe Wrapped in Snow**

A quiet blanket, soft and white,
Cocooning the world in tranquil light.
Every flake tells a story sweet,
As stars in the heavens align in fleet.

Fields of wonder, pristine and pure,
Whispers of magic, of love secure.
Frozen landscapes, silence profound,
In the hush of snow, peace is found.

Beneath the blanket, life awaits,
Dreaming of spring, through frozen gates.
Yet here in winter, stillness thrives,
In snow's embrace, the heart survives.

Crystalline lights dance in the gloom,
A universe spun in winter's womb.
With every breath, the world holds its cheer,
Wrapped in snow, we lose our fear.

So let us wander, hand in hand,
Through this silent, enchanted land.
Where the universe whispers soft and low,
In dreams of winter, forever aglow.

# A Symphony of Stars and Silence

In the canvas of night, stars brightly gleam,
A symphony plays, an immortal dream.
Constellations hum in harmony,
Echoing secrets of eternity.

Each twinkle whispers of tales untold,
Of love and loss, of warmth and cold.
Galaxies swirl in a cosmic dance,
While lovers gaze, lost in a trance.

The silence speaks, a gentle guide,
Through the vastness where wonders hide.
Winds of time carry echoes afar,
Mingling with light of the distant star.

Moonlight bathes the earth in grace,
Every shadow finds its place.
In twilight's grip, we find our fate,
In this symphony, we resonate.

So let us linger beneath the night,
In a world where dreams take flight.
Together we'll weave this melodic chance,
In a symphony of stars, join the dance.

# Under the Gaze of the Glittering Sky

Stars twinkle high, a cosmic dance,
Whispers of dreams in midnight's trance.
Moonlight spills on fields so bright,
Guiding our hearts with gentle light.

Soft breezes carry scents of pine,
Nature's embrace, a sweet design.
In every sigh, the world feels grand,
Under the gaze, we take a stand.

Every heartbeat synced with time,
In this moment, everything rhymes.
The universe sings a lullaby,
As we rest under the sky.

Clouds drift by in lazy grace,
Veiling and unveiling space.
In their shadows, secrets lie,
Woven dreams that dare to fly.

When dawn arrives with golden hue,
The stars give way to skies so blue.
Yet in our hearts, they remain near,
Whispering wishes only we hear.

# Beneath the Hush of Starry Night

Stillness blankets the quiet land,
Crickets sing, as if they planned.
Stars twinkle like diamonds in the dark,
Each one a wish, a hidden spark.

The moon casts shadows, soft and light,
Guiding lost souls through the night.
Beneath this canopy, dreams take flight,
Kissed by the glow, pure and bright.

Time seems to pause in the calm air,
A moment of peace, so rare and fair.
Thoughts drift gently on the breeze,
Wrapped in whispers of ancient trees.

As the night deepens, shadows dance,
Inviting the heart to take a chance.
With every sigh, the world feels right,
Beneath the hush of starry night.

When dawn breaks with a tender sigh,
Memories linger, they never die.
In every heartbeat, the night remains,
A tapestry woven with silver veins.

## Frostbitten Wishes in the Air

Winter's breath brings a silent chill,
Frost on windows, a landscape still.
Whispers of wishes dance in the night,
Caught in the shimmer of pale moonlight.

Snowflakes flutter, each unique in form,
Painting the world, a winter's charm.
Every wish, like a fragile star,
Hopes take flight, no matter how far.

The air is crisp, yet hearts are warm,
Wrapped in memories, a love's true form.
Through the stillness, dreams gently unfold,
In the secrets that winter beholds.

With every step, the crunch beneath,
Echoes of laughter, joy, and wreath.
Frostbitten wishes linger near,
In the heart, they're always clear.

As warm fires crackle and glow,
Stories are shared, and time moves slow.
In this winter's wonder, we dare to share,
All our frostbitten wishes in the air.

## **Echoes of Light in the Snowfall**

Snowflakes whisper upon the ground,
Blanketing silence, a soft surround.
Each flake a echo of light,
Dancing through the gentle night.

In the stillness, memories glow,
Carried by winds that softly blow.
Under the lantern's golden hue,
Light intertwines with silver dew.

Footsteps crunch in rhythmic flow,
Guided by heartbeats in the snow.
Every echo a story told,
Of warmth and love, both brave and bold.

The night sky twinkles with distant stars,
Reminding us of who we are.
In the snowfall, we find our way,
Echoes of light, come what may.

When dawn breaks, the world awakes,
Snowy blankets, the silence it takes.
In echoes of light, we find our peace,
In the gentle snowfall, our hearts release.

## Where Ice Meets the Infinite

In the realm where frost takes hold,
Whispers of secrets, ancient and bold.
The sky stretches wide, a canvas of dreams,
Beneath the gaze of silver moonbeams.

Glacial formations, sharp and bright,
Reflect the shimmer of starlit night.
Time seems to pause, a breath held in awe,
Nature's beauty, without a flaw.

The air, crisp and sharp, makes hearts race,
Each flake a wonder, a delicate lace.
Chilling winds sing of stories untold,
Of souls intertwined, both young and old.

Every shadow dances, every glint gleams,
As the horizon blends with our wildest dreams.
In this frozen expanse, we find our place,
Where ice and infinity embrace with grace.

Under the starlight, we feel so small,
Yet the vastness around us, beckons us all.
Together we stand on this shimmering brink,
Where ice meets the infinite, we pause and think.

## Snowbound Narratives of the Night Sky


Blankets of white cover the ground,
In silence profound, no echoes sound.
The night sky sparkles, a celestial show,
Painting the darkness, a soft silver glow.

Stories unfold in the dance of the snow,
As twinkling stars shyly start to glow.
Winds carry whispers of ages gone by,
Beneath this vast dome, dreams learn to fly.

Each flake that falls tells a tale from afar,
Of journeys and wanderers, each a bright star.
They twirl and flutter, caught in the breeze,
Silent narrators of histories seized.

In this frozen landscape, magic takes shape,
Every moment a promise, each breath a escape.
Through snowbound nights, we find our own way,
Guided by starlight, we wander and play.

As the dawn breaks, hues gently begin,
The night's mysteries fade, but the stories spin.
Snowbound narratives etched in our hearts,
Live on forever though the daylight departs.

## **A Galaxy Draped in Winter's Attire**

Under blankets of snow, the world seems bright,
Stars twinkle gently in the still of the night.
Each flake a marvel, a piece of the whole,
A galaxy dressed in winter, it unfolds.

Mountains rise high, swathed in pure white,
Reaching for cosmos, a magnificent sight.
The universe whispers secrets untold,
In the heart of the frost, treasures unfold.

Skies stretch above in a tapestry spun,
With constellations bright, each a guiding sun.
The chill in the air sings a lullaby sweet,
Where heaven meets earth, every heartbeat.

In this wonderland, dreams drift and glide,
As we wander beneath the cosmic tide.
Each step we take leaves a trace in the night,
A galaxy draped in winter feels right.

Embraced by the silence, our spirits arise,
Connected to all, beneath these vast skies.
In winter's attire, we glimpse the divine,
A cosmic ballet, our hearts intertwine.

## **Ethereal Frost and Starlit Tales**

In the hush of twilight, the frost begins,
Adorning the earth with delicate pins.
Whispers of starlight dance on the ground,
Ethereal treasures in silence abound.

Each spark of light is a story anew,
Of love, loss, and journeys we pursue.
They flicker like dreams in the gateway of night,
Carrying wishes on the wings of light.

The moon weaves a tapestry, soft and serene,
Guiding lost spirits through the spaces unseen.
Frost-laden branches reflect in our gaze,
As we find solace in their exquisite maze.

In the ethereal glow, we share our heartbeat,
With every cold breath, life feels so sweet.
Tales of the cosmos swirl around us,
Wrapped in the magic of winter's soft hush.

Beneath this vast sky where the stories unfold,
We listen to echoes of ages untold.
As starlit dreams whisper deep in our souls,
Ethereal frost embraces, and heals all our holes.

## Storytellers Beneath Frosty Canopies

Whispers travel through the trees,
Tales of wonder on the breeze.
Frosty leaves, a silver crown,
Nature's voice in every sound.

Underneath the frosty skies,
Elder branches stretch and sigh.
Echoes of the past awake,
Memories in every flake.

Gather close, the stories weave,
In this night, we shall believe.
Embers popping, sparks take flight,
Guided by the moon's soft light.

Footprints mark our journey clear,
Every moment held so dear.
With each heartbeat, we unite,
Crafting dreams beneath the night.

Voices meld with winter's chill,
Nature's magic—time stands still.
Frosty canopies embrace,
In the shadows, find our place.

## **Boundless Dreams in a Frozen Realm**

In a realm where silence glows,
Dreams take flight, like falling snow.
Eyes wide open, hearts set free,
Boundless visions wait for me.

Through the night, stars softly gleam,
Guiding pathways of each dream.
Mountains high and valleys deep,
Secrets in the snow, they keep.

Whispers of a world unknown,
In the frost, our hopes are sown.
Every heartbeat, echoing,
In the stillness, dreams take wing.

Gentle breezes, time suspended,
In this space, life's bliss intended.
Frozen smiles and laughter bright,
In this realm, we chase the light.

Each moment blooms, a crystal fresh,
In the snow, we craft our mesh.
Boundless dreams in winter's fold,
Tales of love and joy unfold.

# A Caress Beneath the Milky Glow

Underneath the starlit veil,
Soft caresses, whispers sail.
Moonlit paths where shadows play,
In the night, we drift away.

Gentle breezes in our hair,
Every heartbeat free from care.
Moments stitched with threads of light,
Wrapped in magic, pure and bright.

Crickets sing a lullaby,
As the night unfolds its sky.
Dreams awaken, softly sigh,
In this space, we learn to fly.

With each glance, the world transforms,
In your gaze, my spirit warms.
Milky glow, serene and sweet,
In your arms, my heart's retreat.

Together bound, we make our mark,
In the night, igniting sparks.
A caress that holds the night,
We'll embrace till morning light.

## **Snowflakes and the Infinite Sky**


Snowflakes dance on winter's breath,
Whirling softly, life in death.
Infinite stories in the fall,
Nature's beauty, enchanting all.

As they land, they kiss the earth,
Whispers echo, a sacred birth.
Blankets soft, a cozy sight,
Transforming day into sweet night.

Each flake unique, a fleeting treasure,
Sparkling moments, joy to measure.
Underneath the great expanse,
We find solace in the dance.

Glimmers shine in every flake,
Cast a spell, the world awake.
Infinite sky, the canvas wide,
In this magic, we confide.

Let us wander, hand in hand,
Through this dreamy, jeweled land.
Where snowflakes fall and moments fly,
Underneath the infinite sky.

## **Shimmering Veils of Midnight**

Under the canopy, shadows creep,
Whispers of secrets, the night does keep.
Stars twinkle softly, as dreams take flight,
Wrapped in the glow of shimmering light.

Moonlight spills silver, on tranquil streams,
Painting the world in a soft glow of dreams.
Veils of the night, delicate and thin,
Holding the magic where wonders begin.

The breeze carries laughter, a playful tease,
Through branches that sway with a gentle ease.
Tales of the hearts that wander and roam,
Guided by starlight, they find their way home.

Echoes of river songs softly play,
While shadows with grace join the night's ballet.
In the embrace of the velvet sky,
Every spirit whispers a tender sigh.

In shimmering veils, the night will dance,
Cradling the moment in a celestial trance.
Holding the dreams that the moonlight lends,
Until the dawn breaks, and the magic ends.

## The Dance of Snowflakes and Stars

In the quiet hush of a winter night,
Snowflakes flutter, pure and white.
They twirl like dancers, soft and free,
Joined by the stars in a silent spree.

Each flake unique, a fleeting sigh,
Glistening gently as they drift from the sky.
The earth wears a coat of glimmering frost,
In this magical dance, no moment is lost.

Families gather, hearts aglow,
To witness the beauty of nature's show.
Laughter rings out as snowballs fly,
While winter's enchantment fills the sky.

Frost-kissed dreams in a world so bright,
Every breath clouds in the cool moonlight.
Together they sway in the chill of the air,
A harmony deep, a moment to share.

As morning breaks, the dance doesn't cease,
For in every heartbeat, there's a whisper of peace.
Snowflakes and stars in an eternal waltz,
A tapestry woven, where love never halts.

## Dreams Wrapped in Silver Light

In the stillness, dreams take flight,
Wrapped gently in threads of silver light.
The moon smiles down on every wish,
Soft as a whisper, like a lover's kiss.

Fleeting glimpses of hopes untold,
Dance like fireflies in the night so cold.
Hearts awaken to the magic of night,
Finding their way in the soft twilight.

Every heartbeat tells a story anew,
Of aspirations held and hopes pursued.
With every sigh, a wish will ignite,
Spun from the glow of the starlit night.

Across landscapes where fantasies bloom,
Every shadow reveals a hidden room.
Wrapped in the glimmer of dreams so bright,
Life's wonders unfold, dressed in silver light.

When daylight breaks, the dreams will fade,
Yet in their essence, the night parades.
For in every heart, that silver glow,
Lives on forever, in dreams that flow.

## Night's Bounty of Twinkling Gems

In the velvet embrace of night sky,
Stars emerge like jewels, a wondrous high.
Scattered across the darkness vast,
A treasure of light from a time long past.

Each twinkle tells stories of ancient lore,
Of lovers and warriors, and dreams that soar.
They beckon the gaze of the old and young,
Whispers of verses still yet unsung.

Beneath this blanket, we find our peace,
In the symphony of silence, our worries cease.
Every shimmer a promise, forever held tight,
In night's bounty, all hearts take flight.

Galaxies swirl, with a gentle embrace,
While the moon casts shadows with delicate grace.
In the calm of the night, we seek and we find,
The twinkling gems that light up the mind.

So let us cherish this celestial stream,
With every heartbeat, let us dream.
For in the darkness, we shall not roam,
As night's bounty leads us back home.

## Illuminated by the Celestial Brush

Stars paint the sky with light,
Each twinkle a brushstroke bright.
Night wraps the world in a shroud,
Whispers of dreams softly loud.

Galaxies swirl in cosmic dance,
Hearts lifted in shimmering trance.
The moon's glow, a silver thread,
Guides the lost, where they tread.

Time pauses in the velvet night,
As shadows blend in gentle flight.
The heavens sigh, a lullaby,
Echoing softly, high and nigh.

In this realm, all fears dissolve,
Mysteries of life evolve.
Emotions weave a sacred bond,
In the quiet, of magic beyond.

Awake, the soul bursts into song,
With the stars, where we belong.
Under the celestial brush we find,
Eternal peace, a love entwined.

## Stars Garnishing the Blank Canvas

Night casts a net of endless dreams,
With stars taking shape in silver beams.
A canvas stretched across the sky,
Where wishes drift and hopes can fly.

Each twinkle tells a story vast,
Of worlds unseen, of futures cast.
Galaxies whisper secrets profound,
In the stillness, their echoes resound.

Cosmic tales swirl and bend,
As constellations shift and blend.
Infinity wrapped in a single sight,
A masterpiece born from the night.

Shooting stars, brief miracles bright,
Bring forth memories, a fleeting light.
In the silence, we gather as one,
Under the gaze of the vibrant sun.

The night sky's charm, a sacred art,
Filling the void within each heart.
On this blank canvas, we find our way,
Guided by starlight, to a new day.

## Nightfall's Embrace on Frozen Ground

The sun dips low, casting shadows deep,
Night drapes softly, lulling the earth to sleep.
The air crisp, a blanket of frosty white,
Embracing the world in serene twilight.

Stars emerge, piercing the dark,
Each one a spark, a tiny remark.
Whispers of winter ride with the breeze,
Nature, in slumber, finds perfect ease.

The moon, a guardian, glowing bright,
Shimmers on snow, a soft silver light.
Trees wear diamonds, as crystals cascade,
In the quiet, where shadows fade.

Footsteps crunch on the frozen ground,
With each echo, secrets abound.
Emotions dance in the chilly air,
In nightfall's embrace, we feel the care.

As dreams awaken in the still of night,
Hearts entwined in celestial flight.
Together we gather, in this serene fold,
Sharing the warmth that never grows cold.

## **A Tapestry of Sleet and Starlight**

Beneath a sky of silver fleece,
A tapestry woven in quiet peace.
Sleet falls gently, a soft refrain,
Merging with starlight, a magical stain.

Colors merge in a shimmering blend,
Where winter's chill and warmth transcend.
Each flake a story, each drop a song,
In this woven fabric, where all belong.

The night hums softly with whispers rare,
As nature's breath dances in the air.
A symphony played by the twinkling night,
Guiding lost souls toward the light.

Under the cloak of this celestial weave,
Hearts find solace, and minds believe.
Together we stand, in awe and delight,
Enveloped in whispers of love and light.

In this moment, where shadows glide,
We feel the magic, side by side.
A tapestry spun with stardust bright,
Forever cherished, our hearts igniting.

## **Glimmers Through the Icy Veil**

Soft whispers cross the frozen air,
Icicles hanging, delicate, rare.
Moonlight dances on icy streams,
Nature wrapped in silver dreams.

A tranquil hush, the world holds tight,
Stars glance down, a shimmering sight.
Beneath the frost, life lies in wait,
Hoping for warmth to thaw its fate.

Glistening shards, a crystal display,
Nature's artwork on bright display.
Through the veil, hope begins to peek,
A promise of spring, whispered's bleak.

With every breath, the cold shall fade,
In the heart's warmth, a path is laid.
Glimmers of light, in shadows held,
The icy veil, forever quelled.

## Serenity in the Midnight Chill

Beneath the stars, the world grows still,
Each heartbeat echoes, a quiet thrill.
The night wraps all in a gentle embrace,
With whispers of dreams in this sacred space.

Moonbeams cloak the trees in silver,
The stillness stirs, causing hearts to quiver.
In this chill, worries start to cease,
Moments of solace, embraces of peace.

A breath of night, crisp and clear,
Nature's lullaby, soothing and near.
In shadows long, time drifts slow,
The midnight chill, a tranquil glow.

Close your eyes, let your spirit soar,
In the darkness, find your core.
Serenity wraps the earth like a shawl,
In the midnight chill, we find it all.

## Celestial Reflections on Crystal Waters

Stars above, like diamonds bright,
Glisten softly, a stunning sight.
On crystal waters, they cast their glow,
Whispers of magic, ebb and flow.

Ripples dance in the cool night air,
As if the heavens wish to share.
Each twinkle embraced by gentle waves,
In this tranquil moment, our spirit saves.

Beneath the surface, mysteries dwell,
In every ripple, a story to tell.
Reflections shimmer, dreams intertwined,
Celestial wonders, gently aligned.

The water cradles the sky's soft light,
A mirror of hope in the depth of night.
Celestial reflections, pure and deep,
In crystal waters, love's promise we keep.

## The Quietude of Starry Nights

In the hush of night, a blanket wide,
The stars emerge, a cosmic guide.
Whispers of dreams on the breath of the breeze,
In the quietude, the heart finds ease.

A canvas dark, brushed with light,
Each point a tale, a distant sight.
Beneath this dome, thoughts drift and sway,
Unraveling softly, like clouds of gray.

The stillness here wraps each soul tight,
A moment frozen, pure delight.
In this reverie, worries take flight,
As serenity bathed in silver light.

Look up above, let your spirit gleam,
In the quietude, lose yourself in dream.
Starry nights weave magic anew,
In the solace found, find strength that's true.

**Midnight Reveries Wrapped in White**


The moonlight spills so soft and bright,
A canvas of silence, pure delight.
Whispers of snowflakes dance and spin,
Embracing the night as dreams begin.

In layers deep, the world does sleep,
Each breath a secret, quiet and deep.
Stars peek through the velvet skies,
As fantasies weave, and time softly flies.

A gentle hush, the world confined,
In winter's grasp, the heart aligned.
Moments linger, held so tight,
Wrapped in reveries, lost in the night.

Echoes of laughter float on air,
Memories twinkling, delicate and rare.
In this cocoon of gleaming white,
We find our solace in purest light.

Dreams unfurl like petals wide,
In the arms of night, we softly glide.
Each star a note, each breath a song,
In midnight's reverie, we belong.

## Shining Above the Stillness


The stars are lanterns, cosmic fire,
Illuminating hearts with quiet desire.
Above the world, their glow ignites,
Guiding the lost through endless nights.

A blanket of calm, the earth lies still,
Nature breathes softly, all is tranquil.
In this moment, the universe sings,
With whispers of peace and tiny wings.

The sky's vast canvas, painted bold,
Stories of starlight waiting to be told.
Embers of hope scatter like seeds,
Nurturing life in the heart's deep needs.

Under this dome, dreams take their flight,
Carried on winds adorned with light.
In stillness found, we dare to believe,
That shining above, we never leave.

With every breath, we feel the grace,
In the vastness of time, we find our place.
Together we rise, as shadows fade,
In the brilliance of night, our spirits unmade.

## **Glistening Dreams in the Silent Woods**


In the woods, where silence reigns,
Glistening dreams weave through the veins.
Mossy paths invite the night,
As shadows dance in flickering light.

Stars are the watchmen, quiet and true,
Casting their glow on the forest's view.
Each rustle whispers, secrets concealed,
In the heart of the woods, magic revealed.

A symphony soft, leaves gently sigh,
In a tapestry woven, where spirits fly.
Moonbeams trickle through branches bare,
Bathing the earth in a silver glare.

Here in the hush, where dreams collide,
In the glistening glow, we run and hide.
With nature's breath, life starts to hum,
In the silent woods, our souls become.

Awake in the night, we find our paths,
In the glimmering light, we shed our masks.
The woods will keep our secrets tight,
Embracing the glistening dreams of night.

# The Night's Embrace on Frozen Tides

Frozen tides stretch far and wide,
A mirror of stars in the night's soft glide.
Whispers of waves, like lullabies,
In the night's embrace, where silence lies.

The horizon glows, a painter's brush,
Colors of hope in the gentle hush.
Beneath the stars, the world holds its breath,
In the arms of darkness, there's no death.

Footprints of dreams on icy shores,
Echoes of laughter behind closed doors.
In the still of night, we softly tread,
With hearts unbound, where angels tread.

The moon a lantern, guiding our way,
Through frozen realms where shadows play.
Every whisper of winds, every sigh,
A song of eternity beneath the sky.

Wrapped in starlight, we take our place,
On the frozen tides, we feel the grace.
As night's embrace holds us tight,
We dance through dreams, lost in the night.

## **Secrets Beneath the Moonlight**

Whispers float through the night air,
Hidden tales that few can hear.
Softly glows the silver orb,
Guarding stories wrapped in fear.

Shadows dance on the forest floor,
Cloaked in mystery, they sway.
Every rustle, every sigh,
Hints of secrets kept at bay.

Stars blink high, as if to know,
Of dreams that wander, lost and wide.
In the depths where wishes glow,
Moonlight cradles hearts inside.

A cool breeze stirs the silent trees,
Nature's breath sings soft refrains.
Beneath the moon's watchful gaze,
Love and longing fan the flames.

In every shadow, in every light,
Lies a truth just out of sight.
So listen close when night unfolds,
For secrets shared in quiet holds.

## **Frosted Dreams in Midnight Skies**


The world is cloaked in glimmer bright,
Dreams encased in frosty air.
Stars twinkle like diamonds fair,
Painting wishes on the night.

A soft hush blankets the ground,
Whispers carried far and wide.
Every snowflake, unique and sound,
Hides a tale of joy and pride.

The moon leans low, a watchful friend,
Guiding hearts through shimmering white.
With every breath, the night extends,
Frosted dreams take gentle flight.

In silence sweet, time stands still,
Magic lingers on the breeze.
With every heartbeat, every thrill,
Life unfolds with such great ease.

Beneath the canopy of night,
Hope and wonder softly bloom.
In frosted dreams, we find our light,
As midnight wraps us in its loom.

# **Echoes of the Frozen Cosmos**

In the silence of the stars,
Echoes breathe through icy space.
Whispers of the universe,
Carried on a quiet grace.

Celestial bodies drift and swirl,
Draped in night's cool embrace.
Stories written in frozen dust,
Time etched on a cosmic face.

Galaxies spin with ancient lore,
A tapestry of light and dark.
Each echo speaks of distant shores,
Marking nature's hidden arc.

The vastness hums a lullaby,
To cradle dreams that drift away.
In frozen realms where shadows lie,
The cosmos weaves a bright array.

So when you gaze at the night sky,
Listen close to what it may say.
For within those stars so high,
Echoes of our hearts do play.

# **Radiance Over Glacial Fields**

The dawn breaks with a golden hue,
Illuminating frosted plains.
Glacial fields, a breathtaking view,
Shimmering light from nature reigns.

Each crystalline flake catches the sun,
Transforming cold to warmth anew.
A radiant dance, where rivers run,
And whisper secrets, pure and true.

The air is crisp, alive with cheer,
Birds awaken, songs arise.
In this moment, every fear
Melts away beneath bright skies.

As shadows stretch, the day unfolds,
Life awakens in colors bright.
Within the heart, a story holds,
Of radiance that steals the night.

So walk upon those glacial fields,
Feel the warmth of dawn's embrace.
For in each step, the beauty yields,
A world transformed, a sacred space.

Milton Keynes UK
Ingram Content Group UK Ltd.
UKHW021402081224
452111UK00007B/119